Our Family's
Favorite Grace

TASTE OF HOME readers from across the country sent us their favorite family mealtime prayers so we could share them with *you*. This book is a collection of special graces that have been passed down through generations like treasured heirlooms.

Grandparents share ideas of how they taught their little ones to pray. These lessons of love have helped children learn the importance and meaning of giving thanks.

Page after page, you'll find expressions of gratitude worthy of repeating at your own table. And speaking of gratitude, we'd like to extend ours to all those readers whose names appear after each prayer—they're the ones who made this book possible.

Editor: Cliff Muehlenberg
Associate Editor: Jean Steiner
Art Director: Bonnie Ziolecki
Production Assistants: Ellen Lloyd, Catherine Fletcher
Publisher: Roy Reiman

©2001 Reiman Publications, LLC
5400 S. 60th St., Greendale WI 53129

International Standard Book Number: 0-89821-299-5
Library of Congress Control Number: 00-135496
All rights reserved.
Printed in USA.

For additional copies of this book or
information on other Reiman Publications books,
write: Taste of Home Books,
P.O. Box 990,
Greendale WI 53129-0990; call
toll-free 1-800/558-1013 to
order with a credit card; or
visit our Web Site at
www.reimanpub.com

*C*HAPTERS

I
Daily Graces
Page 5

II
Holiday Graces
Page 139

III
Simple Prayers
For Little Ones
Page 165

Chapter One
Daily Graces

*Berries for the birds,
honey from the bees,
bread on my plate,
Thou givest me.
They sing their song,
I bow my head
and thank Thee, Lord,
for daily bread.*

Marge Boettcher
St. Croix Falls, Wisconsin

We thank You
for the gentle things—
the lamb, the fawn, the dove—
that remind us all
each day we live
of our dear Savior's love.
Please join us at our table and
be our Special Guest;
and may this food and each of us
by Thy grace be blessed.

Jil Giffard
Cedar, Michigan

*Christ in the wilderness
5,000 fed,
with two small fishes
and five loaves of bread.
May the blessings of Him,
Who made this division,
descend upon us
in our provision.*

Elizabeth Curtis
El Paso, Texas

*Bless my little kitchen, Lord,
and light it with Thy love;
help me plan and make my meals
from Thy home above.
The service I am trying to do
is to make my family content;
so bless my eager efforts, Lord,
and make them
Heaven-sent.*

Laureen Lewis
Barrington, Rhode Island

*B*lessed be this feast we share,
Your gracious bounties,
Your love and care.
We praise You, Lord,
for all You give,
so we can please You
as we live.

Gail Rajchel
New Berlin, Wisconsin

*O*ur thanks to Thee
for love that's shared;
our thanks to Thee
for food prepared.
Bless Thou the cup,
bless Thou the bread;
Thy blessing rest upon each head.
Lord, bless us one and all we pray,
as we are gathered here today.

Kathryn Porter
Horsehoe Bend, Arkansas

*O*ur Father in Heaven,
we thank You
for the magic of this life,
for this healthy family,
for the warm sun and for
the quenching rains
that make our crops grow.

Mildred Heck
Arlington Heights, Illinois

*Dear Lord,
You are so good to me,
You give me all life's blessings free:
birds that sing throughout my life;
flowers that bloom
on paths of strife;
a mountainside
where I may roam,
with a winding path
that leads me home;
a sky of every tint and hue.
And then, dear Lord,
You gave me You.*

Erlene Cornelius
Spring City, Tennessee

*For health and food,
for love and friends,
for everything Thy goodness sends,
Father in Heaven,
we thank You.*

Kris Craft
Waterloo, Iowa

*We thank You
for Your goodness, Lord,
Your blessings from above;
and may the meals we prepare
be seasoned with Your love.*

Martha Anderson
Milwaukee, Wisconsin

*From Thy hand
comes every good
and, Lord, we thank Thee
for our daily food.
Over us all
Thy blessings give,
and to Thy glory
may we live.*

Cheryl Bliss
Providence, Rhode Island

*Dear Lord,
we lift our hearts to You
and bow our heads to pray
as we thank You for the blessings
You give to us each day.
And we ask You, Lord,
to guide us
in what we say and do
that we may always walk the path
that leads us home to You.*

Janice Grogan
Cincinnati, Ohio

*O*h You Who clothes the lilies
and feeds the birds of the sky,
Who leads the lambs to pasture
and deer to the waterside;
Who multiplied loaves and fishes
and changed water into wine,
do come to our table
as Giver and as
our Guest Divine.

Harold Seabright
Magalia, California

*We who sit together here,
wish to thank You,
Father Dear,
for Thy love and tender care,
folded round us
everywhere.*

Lois Kaufmann
Holbrook, New York

*Dear Heavenly Father,
I thank You
for this food, this day
and the beauty around us;
I thank You for
the good night's sleep,
the morning light
and the gifts that abound us.
May these and all Your gifts
constantly remind us
of You.*

Floyd Long
Long Beach, California

*As we from Thy bounty eat,
keep us humble, kind and sweet.
May we serve Thee, Lord, each day
and feel Thy love,
Dear Lord, we pray.*

Barbara Jackson
Manahawkin, New Jersey

*We thank You, God, for
families and that we are together;
we thank You
for good things to eat
and for the (season) weather.*

Nancy Anderson
LaBolt, South Dakota

*Father, we thank Thee
for all Thy wonderful and
abundant gifts:
for the gift of life;
for the gift of shelter;
for the gift of food before us;
and for the gift of each other.
We thank Thee
in Jesus' name.*

Paul Gorgos
St. Paul, Minnesota

*Thank Thee,
Heavenly Father,
for Thy blessings one and all,
for the food upon our table—
summer, winter,
spring and fall.*

Lillian Halquist
Denver, Colorado

Lord, we thank You
for Your grace;
our needs are met here
in this place.
We trust You
in Your sovereign way
to lead us closer,
day by day.

Carolyn Goode
Truro Heights, Nova Scotia

*With gratitude
we fold our hands,
with thanks, oh God,
for food and friends and
everything Thy mercy sends.
We ask Thee, Lord,
to be our Guest,
that each one here might be blest
and all may meet in Heaven's rest.
We ask in Jesus' name.*

Winifred Moldenhauer
Pine River, Minnesota

*It was at meals such as this
that Jesus spoke
many of His parables.
Thank You, oh God,
for the opportunity to share
the food of Your Earth
with the food
of our thoughts.*

Susan O'Brien Soucheray
Bayfield, Wisconsin

*Thou Who didst multiply
a little laddie's food
so that it did supply
a hungry multitude,
'tis from Thy hand we feed.
And, Lord, us
thankful
make and
mindful
of the needs
of others, for
Thy sake.*

Sheree Feero
Golden, Colorado

*Lord, send us anywhere,
only accompany us;
place any burden upon us,
only sustain us.
Sever any ties except that which
bind us to Thy heart;
bless this food to the nourishment
of our bodies and our souls
to the service
of Christ.*

The grace used by Robert E. Lee,
shared by W.B. Webster
Wyoming, Ohio

*Oh dearest Lord,
we thank You
for all the gifts You give,
for food and drink and clothing
and homes in which we live.
For parents kind and loving
and friends whose love is true,
tenderly we say,
"We thank You, Lord,
for You!"*

Anna Schall
Mount Laurel, New Jersey

*Blessed Jesus,
be with us
in the breaking of this bread;
with food that
Thou has given may we be fed.
Never leave us when
from this table we do go;
strengthen us for joyful service
with Your light
of love aglow.*

Carole Jensen
White Bear Lake, Minnesota

*D*ear Father in Heaven,
our thanks now we bring
for food
and for clothing
and for every good thing.
Give of Thy blessings
to all who have need,
and help us
to love Thee
in thought, word and deed.

Janet Ashmore
Tampa, Florida

Give us grateful hearts, oh Lord, for food, for health, for friends; be Thou our guide in all we do and keep us to the end.

Arlene King
Rockford, Illinois

*Dear Lord and Father of us all,
forgive us our sins today;
we thank Thee for the food
we have and, then,
Dear Lord, we pray
for friends who can break bread
with us in kindly, loving ways.
For a cozy house built by the road,
and those who pass and say,
"Kind neighbor, we'll come
again," we thank Thee,
Lord, today.*

Bertha Chase
Putnam, Connecticut

Before we eat this food, dear Lord, we bow our heads to pray; for all Thy love and all Thy gifts a grateful thanks we say.

Billie Green
Port St. Lucie, Florida

Heavenly Father, hear our thanks for Thy love and care; help us all to show our love and each blessing share.

Kathryn Bowen
Springfield, Missouri

*God, grant
that in partaking of this food
we may be made
mindful of those who go hungry.
And so strengthen our purpose
that by our daily
deeds of service,
the day may be brought nearer
when no one person may want
for food or fellowship.*

J. Laureen Moran
Regina, Saskatchewan

Again, oh Father,
at Thy call we gather to be fed;
lay hands of blessing on us all
and break our daily bread.

Irmgard Morris
Indianapolis, Indiana

Father, we thank Thee
for this food,
given for our growth and good.
Strengthen us in work and play
and righteous living,
day by day.

Helen Kelly
Longmeadow, Massachusetts

*O*nce again, dear Lord,
we gather
at our family's table.
Once again we thank You, Lord,
for helping us be able
to hear Your voice,
to feel Your love,
to be all that is good.
Please make us worthy every day
of this gift of food.

Greg Wernisch
Highland Park, Illinois

We thank Thee, Lord,
for task and song and food that
makes our bodies strong.
Since our hearts are hungry, too,
we thank Thee, Lord,
for old friends and new.
We also give our thanks to Thee
for meeting with this family.

Marty Hopwood
San Juan Capistrano, California

*Father in Heaven,
sustain our bodies with food,
our hearts with true friendship,
our souls with Thy truth,
for Jesus' sake.*

Gail Knarr
Pittsburgh, Pennsylvania

*Bless this food we share
and the ones who put it there.
Bless those of us
who have aplenty
and share with those
who haven't any.*

Susie Barter
South Pasadena, California

*For daily bread,
for all things good;
for life and health,
for this our food.
For each good gift
Thy grace imparts,
we thank Thee, Lord,
with humble hearts.*

Priscilla Swank
Windham, Maine

*Thank You, Lord,
for this food
that it may nourish my body—
for it is a blessing.
Thank You, Lord,
for Your word
that it may nourish my soul—
for it is a bigger blessing.*

Martha Sabo
Ottawa, Illinois

*Back of the loaf
is the snowy flour,
back of the flour is the mill;
back of the mill is the wheat and
the shower—and the sun and
the Father's will.*

Roberta Werner
Atlanta, Georgia

*For these blessings
from Your store,
keep us thankful evermore.*

Danna Silva
Riverbank, California

*O*ur Heavenly Father,
we thank You today
for Your watchful care over us,
for the blessings You have so freely
bestowed upon us.
We thank You for the food
that we are about to partake,
and we ask You to bless it
to its intended use.
Help us to use the strength it gives
to honor and glorify You.
We ask this in Jesus' precious
name.

Constance Conine
Ladson, South Carolina

*G*ive us, Lord,
a bit of sun,
a bit of work and
a bit of fun.
Give us all in the struggle and
sputter, our daily bread and our
daily butter.
Give us, Lord, a chance to be
our goodly best,
brave, wise and free.
Our goodly best for ourselves
and others,
till all men learn
to live as brothers.

Gwynn Higdon
Owensboro, Kentucky

*Lord, we ask You
to bless this family
with a warm place by the fire
when the world is cold;
a light in the window
when the day is dark;
a welcoming smile
when the road is long;
a haven of love
when the day is done.
For the blessing of this home
and this food,
we give thanks.*

John Wesolowski
Toledo, Ohio

*We thank the Lord
for this our food,
for life and health
and every good.
Bless these, Thy gifts,
and grant that we
with others share
what comes from Thee;
and bless our loved ones
where 'er they be.
For Jesus' sake,
Amen.*

Kassie Cerami
Boise, Idaho

(Join hands)

*We are joined
to give thanks for
which we are blessed,
for the grace to share our fortune,
for the love that we possess.
And thanks for that
which is yet to be,
good food, good friends
and family.
Bless this table and those who
partake of its grain;
bless us in Your holy name.*

Liz Rutledge
Maple View, New York

*Thanks be to Thee
for love that's shared;
thanks be to Thee
for food prepared.
Bless Thou the cup,
bless Thou the bread;
the blessing rest upon each head.*

Mrs. Harold Plumb
Independence, Missouri

*Lord, the gifts Thou dost bestow
can refresh and cheer us, too.
But no gift can to the heart
be what Thou, our Savior, art.*

Gerry Beveridge
Beaufort, North Carolina

*We thank Thee, Lord,
for those daily gifts
we often overlook:
the gift of food
that nourishes our body;
the gift of love
that nourishes our spirit;
the gift of faith
that sustains us;
and the gifts of
family and friends
that comfort us.*

George DeFeis
Waterloo, Iowa

*For peaceful homes
and happy days,
for all the blessings
God displays,
we give Thee
thankfulness and praise,
Who givest all.*

Margaret Fisher
Greenwood, Indiana

*Dear Lord,
once more we call upon
Thy holy name,
realizing that we need Thee.
Bless this food to its intended use,
guide us and direct our life,
and in death save us.
In Jesus' name
we pray.*

Muriel Long
Hemet, California

*Blessed are You,
Oh Lord our God,
Ruler of the Universe,
Who brings forth bread
from the Earth.*

Debbie Noble
Yorktown, Virginia

*For food and health
and happy days,
accept our gratitude and praise.
In serving others, Lord,
may we repay the debt
of love to Thee.*

Eleanor Ruth
Lansdale, Pennsylvania

*Dear Heavenly Father,
bless this food to the nourishment
of our bodies;
bless the hands that have grown
and prepared it. Teach us to be
ever thankful for these
and all Thy many blessings to us,
and guide our lives to Thy service.
In Jesus' name we pray.*

Sadie Rae Hutchinson
Conway, South Carolina

*Come, Lord Jesus,
be our Guest,
and help us with this food
digest.*

Clara Skaarhaug
Greenville, South Dakota

*Oh Lord, to Thee we bring,
Who giveth every lovely thing—
the birds, the flowers,
the sun, the air,
and home and friends and
tender care.*

Deborah Visner
Conover, Wisconsin

For these things we give thanks: for home and friends we hold so dear; for freedom to worship; for life itself. We come to Thee in gratitude and humility.

Zola Houghton
Luray, Kansas

*God, bless this food we eat this day
and keep us well and in Thy way.
And, God, bless this food
we eat this night
and keep us safe
and in Thy sight.*

Lee Knight
Tucson, Arizona

*Our kind and
Heavenly Father,
we thank Thee for the guidance
Thou has given us this day.
Bless this food
which Thou hast placed
before us
that it may be
a nourishment to our lives
and souls as well.*

Beverly Ausman
Elk Mound, Wisconsin

*Father, we thank Thee
for the night
and for the pleasant morning light;
for rest and food and loving care
and all that makes
the world so fair;
to help us to do
the things we should,
to be to others kind and good;
in all we do at work or play,
to grow more loving every day.*

Shirley Byrd
Hickory, North Carolina

*Be present at our table, Lord;
be here and everywhere adored.
Bless these Thy gifts
and grant that we
with others share
what comes from Thee.*

Barbara Walters
Millersville, Maryland

*Come, Lord Jesus, be our Guest;
may our soul by Thee be blessed.
May our soul by Thee be fed,
ever on this living bread.*

Marie Clouse
Hope, Indiana

*May the hearts
of all who eat here
be filled with a love of the Bible
and its teachings.
May all who eat here know
contentment, happiness and peace.
May the Lord watch over us all,
now and always.*

Eric Wooley
Pickerington, Ohio

*Lord, make us
thankful for Thee and
all the blessings we have.
Bless this food;
bless our family.
Forgive us our sins;
help us through this day.
We ask it all
in Jesus' name. Amen.*

Mrs. Lee Kilborn
The Colony, Texas

Gracious God, smile on us in tender mercy. Help us to be humble and truly thankful for these and all other blessings.

Wynell Eley
Gilbert, Louisiana

*Bless this food,
most gracious God,
from Whom all kindness springs;
make clean our hearts
and feed our souls
with good and joyful things.*

Mary Jo Felts
San Bernardino, California

*Thank You, Lord,
for the food we eat;
thank You, Lord,
for the friends we meet.
Thank You, Lord,
for beauty we see;
help us to always
live close to Thee.*

E.B. Fitzgerald III
Gretna, Virginia

*ℋeavenly Father
up above,
we thank Thee
for Thy care and love.
Bless this food before us spread,
and feed our souls
with Heavenly bread.*

Ruth Hutchinson
San Antonio, Texas

*God, thank You
for the food
we are about to receive.
Forgive us our sins and
thank You for all our blessings.
Thank You for the
beautiful day today
and all we've accomplished.
Thank You for our love
for each other.*

Paula Jolliff
Honea Path, South Carolina

God is my help in every need;
God does my every hunger feed.
God walks beside me,
leads the way,
through every moment of the day.
I now am wise, I now am true,
patient, kind and loving, too.
All things I am, can do and be,
through Christ the truth is in me.
God is my health, I can't be sick;
God is my strength,
unfailing and quick.
God is my all, I know no fear,
since God and love
and truth are here.

Barrie Bell
Sonoita, Arizona

*Father, for food before us set
and all other needs
that You have met,
we're truly thankful,
and we'll try
to prove it as each day goes by.
Bless this food to our bodies
and us always to Thy service.*

Judith McMullen
Cloudcroft, New Mexico

Come, dear Lord,
our food to bless;
help us grow in thankfulness.
Lead us, Jesus, in Thy ways;
help us serve Thee all our days.

Char Gast
Colorado Springs, Colorado

We thank Thee, Lord,
for this daily bread,
the blessings on this table spread.
And pray Thee, Lord,
that we may be and do
whatever pleases You.

Joann Suplee
Iverness, Florida

Our gracious Heavenly Father,
we thank Thee for this
and all other manifestations
of Thy loving kindness.
Wilt Thou bless
a portion of this food
for its intended use,
pardon and forgive our
many sins and, at last,
in Christ receive us?

Fran Safarik
Muskego, Wisconsin

Father, for this food we share,
we give Thee thanks
and say a prayer.
That health and strength
we'll surely find,
to feed our hearts, our souls,
our minds.

Marguerite Hosmer
Colorado Springs, Colorado

*L*isten, dear God,
as we now repeat
these words of thanks
for the food we eat.
For all who work
that we may be fed,
we thank Thee,
Giver of daily bread.

Marjorie Thresher
Bolton, Connecticut

*B*e with us, Lord, in breaking
bread, but do not then depart;
abide with us, we pray, and spread
Your table in our hearts.

Marvin Mylander
Wells, Michigan

We thank Thee, dear Lord,
for the hand that feeds us,
for the heart that loves us,
for the wisdom that guides us
and for the grace that forgives us.
Bless this food
for our bodies and us
to Thy service.

Mildred Conover
Dayton, Ohio

*L*ord Jesus, in Thy name
we now,
with grateful hearts,
before Thee bow.
Bless these gifts and grant that we
may always thank and
honor Thee.

Diane Altobelle
Orlando, Florida

*D*ear Heavenly Father,
pardon our many sins
and make us thankful for these
and all other blessings of life.

Wynona Clark
Baton Rouge, Louisiana

*We thank Thee
for this food and for the gifts
of all that's good.
Help us to walk and talk
each and every day
in every kind and noble way.
And may we love
our fellow man
as Jesus loved us all.
Amen.*

John Lee Nicholson
Lerona, West Virginia

$\mathcal{D}$ear Lord,
we consider ourselves
rich beyond words
for having You as our Lord,
our Friend and now
our Honored Guest.
Let all this
fill our heart
with joy, praise
and thanksgiving.

U.K. Nichols
Great Bend, Kansas

*Father, we thank Thee
for our food
and all the blessings of today;
help us to show we thank Thee
by being kind,
we pray.*

Roseann Van Pelt
Springfield, Ohio

*We thank You for this food
and our other blessings, too;
but most of all, dear Lord,
We thank You just for You.*

Margaret Gewalt
West Allis, Wisconsin

*Our kind and precious
Heavenly Father,
we come to You this evening,*
(or approximate time of day)
*thanking You for this food
that is spread here before us.
We ask that it will be used
for the nourishment of our bodies.
We ask You to bless
each and everyone in this home
and to guide and direct us
through this life.
We ask in Thy precious name.*

Maxine Wininger
French, Indiana

*For each hour of each day,
for each minute spent at play,
for the seed You helped us sow,
for the blessed things that grow—
we thank Thee, Lord.
For the roses wild that run,
for the trees that shade the sun,
for the rainbow's brilliant blend,
for the showers that You send—
we thank Thee, Lord.*

For the men who raise the wheat,
for the bread we get to eat,
for the cattle that we need,
for the pastures where they feed—
we thank Thee, Lord.
For our humble small abode,
for the blessings You bestowed,
for the roof that shields the storm,
for the walls that keep us warm—
we thank Thee, Lord.

Brenda Reisch
Howard, South Dakota

We thank You, Lord,
for these gifts we are about to
receive from Your gracious hands.
We pray they will strengthen us
spiritually and physically
to better serve You
and our brothers and sisters.

Kay and Joe Wagner
Dubuque, Iowa

*B*less us now we pray,
for all Thy gifts of this day.
Let our loved ones
that are now with You
know we love and miss them, too.
Let them look down
and be in our hearts,
and stay with us
and never part.
God bless our family on this day,
and know that we are thankful
in every way.

Betty Williams
Joliet, Illinois

Slow us down, God, slow us down. Too seldom do we pause for reflection or to perfect the simple art of doing nothing.

We miss so much in our busyness. Today as we eat, help us to eat slowly, to savor each bite, to cherish as we chew.

Slow us down, Lord, that in our less hurried state we may also be less harried. Remind us to seize the moment, not rush through it.

We thank You for this food and especially the time to eat it.

Amen.

Barbara Davis Taylor
Pebble Beach, California

*T*hank You, Lord,
for bringing us together again.
Bless those who labored in the
fields to produce this bounty.
And never let us forget
that all blessings come from You.
In Jesus' name
we pray.

Erin Hutchinson
Stevens Point, Wisconsin

*Dear Savior,
be our Guest today
in all we do or say.
Bless Thou the food that is set
before us.
May Thy loving care watch over us
and our loved ones,
wherever they may be.*

L.R. Alstadt
Salem, Virginia

*Thou openest Thy hand,
Oh Lord, the Earth
is filled with good;
teach us with grateful hearts
to take from Thee
our daily food.*

Bonnie Foley
Oakhurst, California

*Gracious Lord, smile on us.
Forgive our sins and
remind us to be thankful
for Your countless blessings.*

Norma Smith
Banner Elk, North Carolina

*Dear Heavenly Father,
as we are gathered together
once again to partake
of Thy daily provided food,
knowing it is the work of Thine
hands, how gratefully our hearts
yield thanks. Teach us how to
work and how to live and how to
serve Thee more faithfully. In
Thy name we ask it.*

Sandra Workman
Reading, Pennsylvania

Our Father,
as our heads we bow,
for this food we thank Thee now.
May we truly be true
in all we think and say and do.

Mary Duke
Winnfield, Louisiana

We thank Thee, Lord,
for our food
and for everything that's good.
Guide our feet from day to day
as we walk along life's way.

Dorine Owens
Fulton, Mississippi

*Dear Father in Heaven
from Whom cometh all good
and perfect gifts,
we thank Thee for this food
and for every token
of Thy love.
Grant us grateful hearts
for all Thy benefits,
and feed our souls
with the bread of life.
In Jesus' name we pray.*

Mr. and Mrs. Ed Patten
Milwaukee, Wisconsin

*We thank You, oh Lord,
for this bounty
You have placed before us,
and we pray
that You will also feed
the hunger of our hearts
with the grace
of Your love.*

Bernice Wilkerson
Union Star, Missouri

We thank Thee
for these blessings of food;
we acknowledge them
as gifts from Thy hand.
Help us to use the strength
derived therefrom,
for Thy name's honor and glory.
These things we would ask
in Thy name.

Amy Davis
Troy, Michigan

*Thank You, dear Lord,
for the food
we are about to receive.
Bless our home and
bless all of our loved ones.
Help us be Christian people and
live Christian lives.
Let us bring up our children the way
You would have us bring them up.
Let us be more tolerant of each
other, and let us show our love
to each other more.
These favors we ask
in Christ's name.*

Janice Wilcox
Mulberry, Arkansas

Lord, we ask Your blessing on those who are lonely, as we give thanks for our friends and family gathered here. We ask Your blessing on those who have no shelter, as we give thanks for the warmth of this home. We ask Your blessing on those who hunger, as we give thanks for this bounty before us. Lord, You have promised to meet our needs and for this we are truly thankful.

In Jesus' name.
Amen.

N. Heath
Jacksonville, Florida

Our Father
who art in Heaven, bless these
provisions of Your bounty
now set before us, and feed our
souls with Your bread of life. In
Jesus' name we pray.

Louise Bream
Gettysburg, Pennsylvania

Lord, bless the meat
that we shall eat, the bread
that we shall break;
make all our actions
kind and sweet,
we ask for Jesus' sake.

Barbara Campbell
Marietta, Georgia

*Divine Love
is our bounty;
out of its store we are fed.
Abundance
is poured upon us;
we partake of it in gladness
and acknowledge
these blessings
as children of God.*

Norma Pattison
Dryden, New York

*Father of all, in Heaven above,
we thank Thee for Thy love.
Our food, our home
and all we wear
tell us of Thy loving care.*

Leah Tambolas
Pittsburgh, Pennsylvania

*Be present at our table, Lord;
be here and everywhere adored.
These mercies bless, and grant that
we may be strengthened
for Thy service.*

Melodie West
Palmdale, California

$\mathcal{T}$his is the day the Lord has made,
and each hour will be blessed
if you just ask Him for the strength
to do your very best.
Whatever path you follow,

*He'll be walking by your side
to be your source of comfort,
your friend and constant guide.
The Lord is understanding,
His mercy will not fail;
His love for you is infinite,
His wisdom will prevail.
Remember this each morning,
and you'll not be afraid
to face with growing confidence
the day the Lord has made.*

Dorothy McClintic
Rancho Bernardo, California

*G*od, bless this food.
May it give me strength
to do Your will,
power to be a peacemaker,
energy to bring joy to others
and vitality to love
and be loved.

Carol Doak
Fort Wayne, Indiana

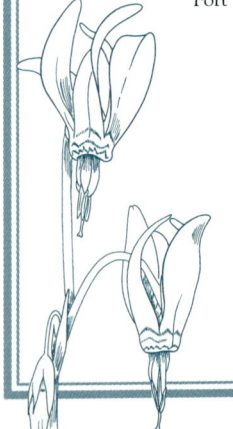

*Lord, we thank You
for all the blessings You have
bestowed upon this family:
for all the days
we have had together
and all the days to come;
for the joys and the sorrows
that bind us ever closer;
for the trials that we've overcome;
and for teaching us
that we can do no great things,
but small things
with great love.*

Diane Mettler
Homewood, Illinois

Again, our Heavenly Father,
we come to Thee with hearts
of praise and adoration,
thanking Thee
for the many blessings of this day.
Forgive us where we have sinned
and come short of Thy glory.
Bless this food
and those who prepared it.
Feed our souls
with the bread of life;
may it strengthen and nourish our
bodies to go forth
in Thy service.

Esther Cavanaugh
Havertown, Pennsylvania

*God is the Head of this house,
the Unseen Guest at every meal,
the Silent Listener
to every conversation.
In the name of Christ,
we bless and give thanks
for this food.*

Theresa Ross
Pueblo, Colorado

*In thanks for the goodness
of days spent together,
we pray that our friends
will be with us forever.
The feelings we share,
the food and good fun,
we pray that God's blessings
have only begun.*

Mary Sathowiak
Pinconning, Michigan

We thank You for our daily food;
our hearts are filled with gratitude.
Oh, hear our prayer and bless
again; in Jesus' name we ask.
Amen.

Carolyn Streight
Yakima, Washington

*G*ive us grateful hearts, dear
Father, and help us to be mindful
of the needs of others.
Amen.

Cynthia Rummell
Landing, New Jersey

Teach me, Father,
when I pray
not to ask for more,
but rather to give thanks
for what is at our door.
For food and drink and gentle rain
and sunny skies above,
for home and friends
and peace and joy,
but most of all for love.

Christine James
Bremerton, Washington

*H*eavenly Father,
from above look down upon
our homes with love.
Keep us in health
and strength each day;
give us our daily bread, we pray.
And for this gift so full and free,
we will return
our thanks to Thee.

Mrs. R.C. Taylor
Crestline, Ohio

*D*ear Heavenly Father,
smile Your love
and kindness down upon us,
and make our hearts
truly grateful for these
and all of our many blessings.
In Jesus' name we ask it.

Vivian Twitchell
Sanford, Florida

Now, *before we eat this food*
we'll not forget
to pray to God,
Who helped us through the night
and brought us to
the morning light.
Help us, Lord, to love
Thee more than we
have ever loved before.
In our work and in our play,
be Thou with us all this day.

Mrs. Robert Wileden
Lansing, Michigan

Our Father in Heaven, help us never to forget Thy love for us. It comes with the light of the morning and remains with the light in the stars of the night. It looks up to us in the beauty of a flower; it shines upon us in the smile of a friend. All beautiful things are the gift of Thy love. Help us to be thankful and to link every beautiful thing to Thee.

Margaret and Leif Dahl
Grand Forks, North Dakota

*T*hank Thee, Lord,
for Thy food,
for life and health
and every good.

Lori Holtz
Brighton, Michigan

'*T*is by Thy truth,
oh Lord, we're fed,
Thy love our every need doth fill;
give us this day our daily bread,
the grace to know—
and do—Thy will.

Margaret Zuber
Marietta, Georgia

*Divine Saviour,
Keeper of our hearts,
remind us always
of Your holy presence.
Teach us to recognize
and, therefore, be grateful
for the blessings
You so generously grant us
every day. And most of all,
help us to be worthy
of Your love.*

Pauline Dunn
West Allis, Wisconsin

We thank Thee, Lord,
for happy hearts,
for rain and sunny weather;
we thank Thee, Lord,
for this our food
and that we are together.

Arlene Donnell
Springfield, Missouri

As we partake of earthly food,
the table before us spread,
we'll not forget to thank You, Lord,
Who gave us daily bread.

Grace Mueller
Sonoma, California

*For food and all
Thy gifts of love,
we give Thee thanks
and praise;
look down, oh Father,
from above
and bless us all our days.*

Priscilla Weaver
Hagerstown, Maryland

*W*hat God gives
and what we take,
'tis a gift for Christ, His sake.
Be the meal of beans and peas,
God be thanked for
those and these.
Have we flesh or have we fish,
all are fragments
from His dish.

Judy Mae Thiel
Miller, South Dakota

*With home and health
and happiness,
we wouldn't want to fuss;
for by this stack of evidence,
God's been good to us.*

Sherri Horonjeff
Acton, Massachusetts

𝒟ear Lord,
give us health enough to make
work a pleasure; wealth enough to
support Your needs; strength
enough to battle difficulties;
grace enough to overcome sin;
patience enough to toil so You can
accomplish; charity enough to see
good in others; faith enough to
make real the things of God;
hope enough to remove
all fear of the future.

Emily Hoy Fields
Santa Ana, California

*We thank Thee, Lord,
for daily bread,
and while our bodies thus are fed,
may we serve with heart and hand,
doing always Thy command.*

Karen Strate
West Valley City, Utah

*For home, love and all things true,
we give our thanks,
dear Lord, to You.
In Jesus' name we pray.
Amen.*

Katie Nelson
Ruston, Louisiana

*For the silver rain
and the shining sun and fields
where scarlet poppies run.
For all the ripples of the wheat
are in the bread that I do eat.
So when I sit for every meal
and say my grace,
I always feel
that I am eating rain
and sun and fields
where scarlet
poppies run.*

Phyllis Horal
Vancouver, Washington

Father, we thank Thee
for this wonderful day,
for all our blessings
along life's way.
Guide us,
protect us
and forgive all our sins,
and be ever present
as this meal now begins.

Marilyn Bird
Asbury, New Jersey

*Bless this kitchen,
Lord, we pray,
the food we eat and
the things we say.
Give us the strength
to do our tasks,
and help us remember
Thou are first
and we are last.*

Christine Varner
Washington, DC

As You blessed
the loaves and fishes,
bless the food upon our dishes.
Like the sugar
in our tea,
may our lives
be stirred by Thee.

Wonda Miller
Wenatchee, Washington

*A*ccept our gratitude,
dear Lord, for all the blessings
Thou dost give;
direct and guide our daily path,
and teach us how to live.

Jere Jensen
Metuchen, New Jersey

*T*his is our food,
dear Lord, indeed,
given for our daily need.
Take our thanks we pray,
and guide us through
another day.

Renetta Sargent
Indianapolis, Indiana

We thank Thee
for our daily bread;
let also, Lord, our souls be fed.
Oh bread of life, from day to day,
sustain us
on our homeward way.

Inez Romer
Virginia, Minnesota

*Before we eat
we bow our heads,
bless this milk and bless this bread.
Bless our father and our mother,
and keep us close to one another.
Bless all children far and near,
keep them safe and free from fear.
Bless our family and our friends,
and keep us happy
till this day ends.*

Ruth Lindhart
DeKalb, Illinois

(Breakfast)
Gracious Giver of all good,
Thee we thank for rest and food.
Grant that all we do or say,
in Thy service be this day.

(Lunch)
Father, for this noonday meal,
we would speak the praise we feel.
Health and strength
we have from Thee;
help us, Lord, to
faithful be.

(Dinner)

*Tireless Guardian of our way,
Thou hast kept us well this day.
While we thank Thee, we request,
care continued, pardon, rest.*

Dorothy Lambertsen
Portland, Oregon

(Before dinner)
Come, Lord Jesus, be our Guest,
and may these gifts to us be blest.

(After dinner)
Lord Jesus,
Thou hast been our Guest;
we thank Thee
for this food so blest.
Oh, may Thy grace to us be given,
one day to be Thy guest
in Heaven.

Carol Spomer
Lafayette, Colorado

*Fold your hands
and let us pray,
thanking God for this nice day.
Thank You for the friends we meet;
thank You for the food we eat.
Thank You for another day
of love that's shared
in many ways.*

Sally Grushon
Kalamazoo, Michigan

(Sung to the melody of "Praise God from Whom All Blessings Flow")

*Be present at our table, Lord;
be here and everywhere adored.
Thy people bless, and grant that
we may feast in paradise with Thee.*

Carol Anne McCreary
Mount Ayr, Iowa

(Sung to the melody of "Michael Row the Boat Ashore")

*Come, Lord Jesus, be our Guest;
Hallelujah.
Let these gifts to us be blest;
Hallelujah.*

Jamie Anheuser
New Bern, North Carolina

(Sung to the melody of "Edelweiss")

Bless our lives, bless our homes, bless our every endeavor;
warm us all with Your love
and our love for each other.
Friendship and joy, may they
fill our hearts,
thankfulness forever;
bless this food, precious Lord,
as we eat it together.

Kathryn Hillen
Cedar Falls, Iowa

*O*h, the Lord is good to me.
And so I thank the Lord
for giving me the things I need—
the sun and the rain
and the apple seed.
Oh, the Lord is good to me.

Darcie Turpin
Gainesville, Georgia

*G*od doth supply our every need;
He doth our every hunger feed.
He walks beside us
and guides our way,
through every moment
of every day.

Mildred Cook
Rocky River, Ohio

*W*e pray Thee bless this
food and keep our bodies strong;
help us, Lord, to live for
You the whole day long.

Vernita Coffey
Grandview, Washington

*Father, we thank Thee
for this food;
pray Thee bless it to our good.
Keep us, love us, every day;
may we from Thee
never stray.*

H. Wayne Hammond
Darlington, Pennsylvania

*Dear Lord, we look upon the
fields and see Your plenty there;
You have blessed us with this food,
we thank You for our share.*

Marilyn Buer
Hales Corners, Wisconsin

*O*n our farm,
from field to table,
let us eat as we are able.
Thanking God, the Lord above,
as we share our food
with family love.

Pam Hansberger
Norwalk, Ohio

*For food and health
and happy days,
accept our gratitude and praise.
In serving others, Lord,
may we repay
our debts of love
to Thee today.*

Kay Ward
Springfield, Vermont

*Thank You now
for the food to eat,
for fresh clean water to drink.
I thank You, too, for rest and care
and little children everywhere.*

>   Pauline Dabek
>   Horseheads, New York

*God, we thank You for this food;
help us appreciate it as we should.
Please help others, also we pray,
to have the food they need today.*

>   Effie Brown
>   London, Kentucky

God, we thank You
for our food,
for health and all things good,
for wind and rain and sun above,
but most of all
for those we love.

Daniel Dietrich
York, Pennsylvania

We thank You, Lord,
for daily bread
and all the blessings on us shed.
We pray Thee guard us
with Thy love
and guide us to Thy home above.

Roberta Matt Traviss
Des Moines, Iowa

Heavenly Father, we do pray
that You'll bless this food today.
Bless this family gathered here
and all the ones they hold dear.

Jane Harter
Nazareth, Pennsylvania

God, bless not only
food and drink,
but what we do and what we think.
Grant that in our work and play,
we might love Thee more each day.

Penny Wegher
Custer, South Dakota

*Thank You, Lord,
for the morning light,
for this day
so fresh and bright.
For health and strength
and loving care,
we thank You for
this food we share.*

Gertrude Teitsmas
Hudsonville, Michigan

ℒord Jesus, be our Guest,
our morning joy, our evening rest.
And with our daily bread impart
Thy love and peace
to every heart.

Mathilda Murphy
Meadville, Pennsylvania

ℱor all we eat
and all we wear,
for daily food and nightly care,
we thank Thee, Heavenly Father.

June Drew
Ithaca, New York

*O*ur Father,
we thank Thee for this food,
remembering those who are hungry.
We thank Thee for our health,
remembering those who are ill.
We thank Thee for our homes,
remembering those who are homeless.
We thank Thee for our friends,
remembering those who are friendless.
We thank Thee for these blessings,
and ask Thee to bless
those who go without.

Emma Streenz
Aberdeen, South Dakota

Chapter Two
Holiday Graces

Special-Occasion Graces

Father, we thank You for the wonderful family gathered here today. We thank You for Your blessing and the bounty You have bestowed on us, symbolized by this table and this gathering. We thank You for the laughter of children heard here today. We pray You guide them as You have guided us. May they come to know and appreciate the strength and comfort You offer.

Tom Martin
La Grange, Illinois

*Lord, on this most special day,
please bless our family's food;
bless our happy home and hearth
and all things that are good.
Bless our friends who share with us
this bounty as we pray;
and thank You, Lord, for granting
us the blessing of this day.
Amen.*

Steve Snyder
Brookfield, Wisconsin

*B*lest are You, Lord,
God of our fathers.
Through Your goodness we enjoy the
fruits of the Earth and share the loving
gifts of family and friendship.
We ask Your blessings on our guests,
our table and our home.
We offer thanks for the love with which
this festive meal was prepared,
and for the love and joy which brings us
together to partake of it.
In gratitude for Your continued care over
us, make us mindful of
the needs of others

*that we may show our thanks
in the manner of our living.
May our hearts be filled with love and
praise as we pray to Your holy name.
Amen.*

Eileen Chaney
Elizabeth City, North Carolina

*B*less the family living here;
draw them close with love and cheer.
Bless the food that's been prepared;
bless the guests
with whom it's shared.
Bless us all that ever we,
may live, oh Lord, with Thee.

Mary Neuroth
Baldwinsville, New York

*We thank You, Lord,
for the food we eat—
for bread and cheese and
milk and meat;
for sugar, salt and savory spice,
for apple pies, cakes and rice.
But, Lord, we thank You
most of all
for warmth of friends who
come to call
to share our bread,
our cup of cheer,
for friendship's always
welcomed here.*

Philip Grazide
Santa Rosa, California

Easter Graces

*Easter is here,
the board is spread;
thanks be to God
Who gives us bread.*

Evelyn Proffit
Mason, West Virginia

*We thank You, Lord,
for Jesus Christ
and for the blood He shed;
we thank You for His risen life
and for our daily bread.*

Branette Richards
Sequim, Washington

*Risen Savior,
be present with us
at this Easter celebration.
Keep us always mindful that
You opened the gates of Heaven
so we may one day be with You.
Let our strength and
spirit be restored
that we may serve others
as You have shown us
how to serve.*

Niel Foxx
Lawrence, Kansas

Thanksgiving Graces

*Lord, behold our family here
assembled. We thank Thee for
this place in which we dwell;
for the love that unites us;
for the peace accorded us this day;
for the hope with which
we expect the morrow;
for the health, the work, the food
and the bright skies that make our
lives delightful; for our friends in
all parts of the world.*

Jeanette Block
Vashon Island, Washington

(Join hands)

*Beloved Creator,
we bow our heads and
join our hands
at this Thanksgiving table
to honor You,
to adore You and
to thank You
for all Your countless blessings
and the bounty You have placed
before us today.*

Rosemary Richardson
Bay View, Wisconsin

Be Thou our Guest, dear Lord, at this Thanksgiving dinner. As we enjoy the fruits of Thy bounty, may our souls be refreshed by Thy presence and peace.

As we leave this table, may we be strengthened physically as well as spiritually in Thy dear name's sake.

Janet Faulhaber
Madison, Wisconsin

*This is a special day we all give
thanks to the Lord above.
We thank Him for the things we
usually take advantage of:
Thank You for our friends
and families, and thank You for
helping us through our difficulties;
Thank You for guiding us through
thick and thin, and thank You
for making us realize that before
perfection comes discipline;
Thank You for our lives,
food and land, and thank You
mostly for being there
when we need a helping hand.*

Jo Wells
Comstock, Nebraska

*Thank You, Lord,
for the gift of love;
thank You for blue skies above.
Thank You for the good health
we've had and for being together
at Thanksgiving,
which makes us glad.
Thank You for the food we eat;
thank You for the people we meet.
Thank You for friends
big and small;
and, Lord, please bless us,
one and all.*

Carol Thompson
Leicester, New York

*ℬless our family
gathered here;
thank You for another year.
Grateful for the joy of living,
we thank Thee, Lord,
for this Thanksgiving.*

Edna Devecis
Ashburnham, Massachusetts

*L*ord, we humbly ask Thy blessing
on the turkey and the dressing,
on the yams and the cranberry jelly,
and the pickles from Aunt Nelli.
Bless the pumpkin pie and tea;
bless each and every calorie.
Let us enjoy Thanksgiving dinner;
tomorrow we can all get thinner.
For all Thy help along the way,

*we're grateful this
Thanksgiving Day.
We're thankful, too,
for all our dear ones—
for all the far away and near ones.
Although we may be far apart,
we're together in our hearts.
Keep us in Thy loving care;
this is our Thanksgiving prayer.*

Mary Jane Muehlenberg
Milwaukee, Wisconsin

*Just as the Pilgrims thanked
You, Lord, for all you did
for them, so today we bow
our heads and thank You, too.
Amen.*

Lenora Rhyner
Green Bay, Wisconsin

*For nuts and pears and apples,
for everything we need,
for pumpkin pie and turkey,
we give Thee thanks, indeed.*

Jeri Ruser
East Fallowfield, Pennsylvania

Christmas Graces

*Let not our hearts be empty inns
that have no room for Thee,
but cradles of the living Christ
at His nativity.*

Melda Marson
Orillia, Ontario

*Thank you, Lord, for all You
have given to us: for this feast, for
our gifts, for our health and
especially for the gift of love we all
share on this, Your holy birthday.*

Barbara Fead
Cincinnati, Ohio

For love of family and friends and all the gifts Thy mercy sends, Father in Heaven, we thank Thee. And for the greatest gift of all—a Savior born in a stall—Father in Heaven, we thank Thee. Our Father, help us to keep in mind the spirit of Christmastime and the happy songs the angels sang on that first Christmas night.

Susie Pratt
Bristol, Virginia

Holy God, as we bow our heads before You, help us make room at the inn within us. Help us welcome Christ's light shining from the Christmas tree, Christ's warmth radiating from the hearth and Christ's presence lingering at our table. We ask Your blessing upon this food as we open the door within us beckoning. Yes. There is room. There is room at the inn.

Adel Crum
Peoria, Illinois

Birthday Graces

For Mother

Heavenly Father, we gather together to honor our mother on her special day and to thank You for Your gift of blessing us with her. Help us to show others Your love as she has shown us, with gentle words and simple kindness. And bless this meal which we are about to share.
Amen.

Nancy Miller
Covington, Kentucky

For Father

$\mathcal{D}$ear God and Father of us all, we are grateful for all Your blessings, especially the father You sent to love us.
For we needed his advice when we thought we didn't, we needed his strength when we could do it alone, and we needed his humor when there was nothing to laugh about. Bless him on this, his special day. Amen.

Andy Dufford
Evanston, Wyoming

Birthday Graces for All

*The candles glow
upon this cake
to symbolize each year
that You have given me, dear Lord,
to live through without fear.
For I will keep inside my heart
Your gifts of hope and love;
You are the flame
that lights my path,
my candle from above.*

Bonnie Ziolecki
Menomonee Falls, Wisconsin

*𝒟ear God,
please let some blessings
fall on each one here—
large and small.
And since this is (name)'s
special day,
please bless (him/her)
in Your special way.*

Gerry Ebert
Milwaukee, Wisconsin

Wedding Grace

*Come, Lord Jesus, be our Guest;
let this food to us be blessed.
Blessings on the bride and groom
and everyone in this room.
Guide them safely on their way
from this, their happy
wedding day.*

Jean Elvers
Red Deer, Alberta

Chapter Three
Simple Prayers for Little Ones

*Little children
all are we,
bow our heads unto Thee,
thanking You for all unveiled
as we travel life's short trail.
Bless our food here on Earth,
nourished bodies
waiting new birth.*

Irene Dunn
Milwaukee, Wisconsin

*For colors
in the food we eat,
for aromas
that smell so good,
for things
to taste and things to see,
for Mommy, Daddy
and for Thee,
Father in Heaven,
we thank Thee.*

Jane Kitson
Lawrenceville, Georgia

*Bless us
with this food to eat;
bless us with the friends we meet.
Bless us with Your precious love;
guard us, Jesus, from above.
Oh, sweet Lord,
You are my way;
thank You, Jesus,
for today.*

Shannon MacMurtrie
Falls Church, Virginia

*Although he is too
small to pray
and thank You
in the proper way,
bless his peas
and bless his meat
and everything
he tries to eat.*

Shelly McCallum
Alymer, Ontario

*To thank Thee, Lord,
I bow my head
for golden butter on my bread;
for fruit and milk
so fresh and sweet,
for all that makes
this meal complete.*

Gloria Johansen
Ryder, North Dakota

*T*hank You, God,
for daily bread,
for oranges and apples red;
for milk and cookies
and special treats,
for all the things good to eat;
for meat and eggs
to make us strong,
thank You, God,
the whole day long.

Mrs. Charles Scharver
Massillon, Ohio

*F*or every cup and every plateful,
please make us truly grateful.

Emily and D.J. Gaulke
Pewaukee, Wisconsin

I see a garden rosy and fair,
with things growing everywhere.
God feeds the little birds and me;
my thanks and love
I give to Thee.

Leo and Marlene Redding
Gettysburg, Pennsylvania

*Thank You, God,
for milk and bread,
for warmth of fire
and warmth of bed;
for lighted lamps, for gentle care,
for these small hands
held in prayer.*

Elaine Ketner
Ionia, Michigan

*Thou openest Thy hand,
Oh Lord, and our table is filled.
Bless us ever
with grateful hearts.*

Amy Cunningham
Oklahoma City, Oklahoma

*We love our bread,
we love our butter;
most of all we
love each other.*

Patty Adolphs
Madison, Wisconsin

*D*ear Father in Heaven,
we thank Thee for this day,
for food and for clothing,
for work and play.
Now help us so kindly
to do what is right
and keep us from quarreling
till bedtime tonight.

Stella and Michael Laursen
Clearwater, Florida

*I thank Thee,
dear Father
in Heaven above,
for Thy goodness and mercy,
Thy kindness and love.
I thank Thee for home,
friends and parents so dear,
and for every blessing
that I enjoy here.*

Toshie Shishido
Haiku, Hawaii

*Our hands we fold,
our heads we bow;
for food and drink,
we thank Thee now.*

Irene Whatling
West Des Moines, Iowa

*Bless me, Lord,
from my head to my feet;
now bless this food
we're about to eat.*

Deborah Shifferly
Canton, Ohio

Great gray elephants,
little tiny bees,
pretty purple violets
and tall green trees—
God gave all these things to me,
and He gave me two eyes
so I could see.
Thank You, God,
for everything that
You've given me.

Kathy Walsh
Cincinnati, Ohio

𝒴ou are to me, Oh Lord,
what wings are to the bird.

> Pat Commons
> Aultman, Ohio

ℱor flowers that bloom
about our feet,
for tender grass so
fresh and sweet,
for the food we are about to eat—
Father in Heaven,
we thank Thee.

> Callie Houx
> Magnolia, Arkansas

*Thank You
for the food
we are about to receive.
Forgive us our sins.
Thank You for all the blessings
of this beautiful day
and all that we've accomplished.
And thank You
for our love
for each other.*

Paula Jolliff
Honea Path, South Carolina

*Every time
I eat my meals
I thank my Lord above,
Who made my food and blessed it
from His kind heart of love.
I fold my hands
and thank Him,
I know He hears
my prayers;
the food we have
reminds me
that Jesus
really cares.*

Lee and Sherri Terry
Lynden, Washington

*Thank You, God,
for love and care;
thank You, God,
for the clothes we wear.
Thank You for our homes and food;
You are always kind and good.
Thank you for our
strength and health;
thank You for our
country's harvest wealth.
Thanks for love, life and joy;
and thank You from
every girl and boy.*

Sandra McKibben Towns
Fort Lupton, Colorado

*$\mathcal{T}$hank You, God,
this happy day,
for food and home and
friends and play.*

Susan DeBay
East Granby, Connecticut

*$\mathcal{D}$ear God,
for this food that makes us grow,
and because You love us so,
we thank Thee.*

Mrs. Jack Walker
Walland, Tennessee

*For this food
upon our table,
for the birds outside our door,
we thank Thee,
Heavenly Father,
for these things
and
many more.*

Donna Bugyi
Easton, Pennsylvania

*G*od, we thank You
for our food
and for Your tender care;
how good of You to love us all,
everyone, everywhere.

> Emma Schaefer
> Emporia, Kansas

A,B,C,D,E,F,G,
thank You, God,
for feeding me.

> Patti Hitchcock
> Tennille, Georgia

*God is great.
God is good.
God is in our neighborhood.*

Linda Allton
Wellington, Kansas

*Dear Lord,
we thank You for this food
as well as we are able;
please bless it, Father, to our use
and be with us at the table.*

Linda Ramsey
Westport, Washington

*Father, we thank Thee
for every happy day,
for trees and flowers,
for sunshine and play,
for our homes in America
and our kind parents, too.
All these things
we're thankful for,
but most of all,
for You.*

Phyllis Braud
Baton Rouge, Louisiana

*Dear Lord,
our thanks we say
for home and food and all things
good You give to us each day.*

Connie Smith
Covington, Kentucky

*God, bless the food before us
here, for those with whom we
share it, for the
ones who helped to
grow, to harvest
and prepare it.*

Dorothy Whitcomb
Binghamton, New York

*Dear Father in Heaven,
we give Thee our praise;
may all little children be kind
in their ways.
We ask Thee for food,
which we need every day;
forgive us when we have been
cross in our play.
We know Thou art loving
and always the same;
we ask this in dear
Jesus' name.*

Grace Lowe
Hamilton, Ohio

We who sit together here
wish to thank You, Father Dear,
for Thy love and tender care,
folded round us everywhere.

Lois Kaufmann
Holbrook, New York

*B*less us, Lord,
and bless this food;
keep us in a happy mood.
Bless the cook and all who serve
us—and from indigestion,
Lord, preserve us.

Caroline Chiarello
Newbury Park, California

*Thank You
for the food we eat,
for those who share or serve it.
And if there be a good dessert,
grace us to deserve it.*

Helen Hall
Pickering, Ontario

*Three potatoes for
the four of us—
thank the Lord
there ain't no more of us.*

Elizabeth Sause
Staten Island, New York

*We thank the Lord
for food and drink,
for appetite and
power to think,
for loved ones dear,
for home and friends,
for everything
the Good Lord sends.*

Kim Ludiker
Borger, Texas

*Thank You, Father,
for this food
and for this time we share
with those we love.*

Margaret Dodge
Cuyahoga Falls, Ohio

*We wish for food,
peace and happiness for all the
children in the world.
Amen.*

Barbara Heimer
Woodbury, Minnesota

*B*less our food
and drink, dear Lord,
and bless our little friends, too;
help us day by day to show
our love and thanks
to You.

Rachel Adams
Limestone, Maine

*H*ere is love and here is bread;
thank you, God, we are
all well fed.

Zola Ashley
Pukwana, South Dakota

*G*od, bless this food
we now enjoy
to make our bodies strong;
help us to remember that
to You we do belong.

Janice Charton
Tallmadge, Ohio

*Thanks for food
that helps us grow,
for family and friends
that we know.
Thanks for all the world we see;
thank You, God,
for loving me.*

Debbie Kohany
Valhalla, New York

Dear Lord,
we thank Thee for Thy care
and for this gift
of food to share.

Jennifer Boyd
Chicago, Illinois

As I walk up to the table,
I see the good food there;
I thank my Heavenly Father
before I take my share.

Joan Burnet
Greensboro, North Carolina

*Accept our gratitude,
dear Lord, for all the blessings
Thou dost give;
guide and direct our daily paths
and teach us how to live.*

Shirley Titus
New Hope, Pennsylvania

*Bless this food,
bless our friends,
bless our moms and dads.
Amen.*

Cindy Pletcher
Stratton, Colorado

*May all that we do
and all that we say
help to brighten another's day.
And may this meal
give strength today
to do Your will
at work and play.*

Sharyn Holcomb
St. Paul, Minnesota

*Dear Jesus,
we are thankful
for all the things
You give us every day.
Please bless us, keep us happy,
make our thoughts good,
our words gentle, our actions kind
and make me a big help
to Mom and Dad.*

Danielle Evert
Pewaukee, Wisconsin

Come, dear Lord,
and be our Guest;
the food Thou gave us
by Thee be blessed.

May Salisbury
Auburn, California

For all Your goodness, Lord,
we give You thanks:
for the food we eat,
for the friends we meet,
for each new day we greet,
we give You thanks.

Linda Wagner
Pueblo, Colorado

*Dear Jesus,
thank You for the sun above;
thank You for Your endless love.
Thank You for this food so good;
please help us do
the things we should.*

Angie Zangs
Rochester, Minnesota

*We bow our heads
and close our eyes to say,
may every little child on Earth
be fed today.*

Janet Harden
Brunswick, Georgia

*G*uide me, Jesus, in all I do;
help me to be kind
and good and true.
Show me how to give and share
and love all people everywhere.

Chris Devine
Janesville, Wisconsin

*O*ur hands we hold,
our heads we bow,
for food and drink
we thank Thee now.

Irene Whatling
West Des Moines, Iowa

*My dear
Jesus from above,
thanks for this house
and those I love.
Everything is a gift from You,
so thank You for
this good food, too.*

Jeffrey & Nikki Condit
Pewaukee, Wisconsin

*For health and strength
and daily food,
we give Thee thanks,
oh Lord.*

Ruth Proksch
Iron River, Michigan

*Dear God, we thank You
for this meat
and seemly things to eat;
for milk that's cold
and soup that's hot—
please make us happy with our lot.*

Mrs. William Murphy
Minersville, Pennsylvania

*𝒟ear Lord,
for this gift of food
we bow our heads in gratitude.
And from our
thankful hearts we pray
that we do Thy will today.*

Linda Schierman
Vulcan, Alberta

*B*less this meat
that we shall eat,
this bread that we shall break;
make all our actions
kind and sweet,
we ask for Jesus' sake.

Dawn Tetirick
Monument, Colorado

*B*efore we eat
we bow our heads
and thank our God for
our daily bread.

Cathy Knutson
Marion, Ohio

*As we gather
near this table round,
let no unhappy soul be found.
Bless us through the day
and guide us in Your perfect way.
In Your holy name we pray.*

Jane Johnson
Woodland, Texas

*Lord, thank You
for the food before us,
the friends beside us
and the love between us.*

Arla Albers
Fairfax, Virginia

*Dear God,
in my little heart I know
that You gave me this food,
and I love You so.
I want to tell You now, thank You
'cause I know in my heart
that You love me, too.*

Jacob Gaulke
Pewaukee, Wisconsin

*Thank you, God,
for my brothers and sisters,
Mom and Dad,
grandpas and grandmas.
Thank You for a house to live in,
a yard to play in, a school to learn
in, for summer vacation
and, oh yeah, for Christmas.
And thanks for this food,
whatever it is,
and someone to cook it for us.
God bless us all.*

Erin Grolsch
Aberdeen, Washington

*Oh my God,
I give You this day,
all that I think and all that I say.
I give you my love
with Jesus Your Son;
today I will try
to love everyone.*

Madelyn Redding
Donnybrook, North Dakota

*Thank You for our food
that makes our bodies strong
and helps to keep us well
all day long.*

Betty Nundalh
Oakes, North Dakota

*For food, drink and loving care,
for friends and gladness everywhere.
We thank Thee,
Father, kind and good,
help us to love Thee
as we should.*

Virjean Willock
Terre Haute, Indiana

*Teach me to be thankful, Lord,
in everything I do;
for all the things I call my own
are really gifts from You.*

Emily Guirlinger
Pewaukee, Wisconsin

*Come, Lord Jesus, be our Guest;
let these gifts to us be blessed.
A thousand thanks shall be,
dearest Jesus, unto Thee.*

Susan Myck
Drayton Valley, Alberta

*For the hand that guides us,
for the heart that loves us,
for the grace that saves us,
we thank Thee, Lord.*

Bill Chaffee
Lexington, Kentucky

*Sit with us, Silent Guest,
a friend indeed we love best.
May Thy presence make us feel
pure happiness
throughout this meal.*

Gladine Fiksdal
Watertown, South Dakota

*Jesus, dear Friend,
hear me pray;
be our Dinner Guest today.
Stay with us,
be always near;
bless all those who enter here.*

Nancy Robjohns
Wauwatosa, Wisconsin

*Father in Heaven,
softly we pray;
we wish to say thank You,
just for today.*

Arvetta Harley
San Antonio, Texas

*Thank You
for the world so sweet;
thank You
for the food we eat.
Thank You
for the birds that sing;
thank You, God,
for everything.*

Miriam Spengler
Bath, Pennsylvania

*It's hard to wait
for grace
when you're hungry
as a bear;
but everything
tastes better
when you say
a thank-you prayer.*

Nancy Kane
Chalfont, Pennsylvania

*Bless, oh Lord,
these delectable vittles;
may they add to Your glory
and not to our middles.*

Cora Sue Howe
Rome, New York

(Prayer before leftovers)
*Heavenly Father,
bless this food and the hands
that have repaired it.*

Dot Williams
Colorado Springs, Colorado

*O*h Lord,
please make us able
to eat all that's on the table.
Any more that's still in the pot—
bring it on while it's still hot.

Dot Donohoe
Huntington, West Virginia

*T*hank You
for this meal abundant;
and thank You, God,
for Mom—she done it!

Rebecca Jones
Washington, D.C.

(Join thumbs and index fingers, forming circles, and put over eyes to make glasses.)

There are many things I'm grateful for; I can see them near and far.

(With both hands, make a ball and hold it high over your head to form the Earth.)
I am thankful for the Earth.

(Move hands in front of your chest to make waves.)
I am thankful for the sea.

(Place hand on a friend's shoulder.)
I am thankful for my friends.

(Cross arms over your chest.)
I am thankful to be me.

Amen.

Edye Cloud
Glenwood Springs, Colorado

I wiggle my fingers,
I wiggle my toes;
I wiggle my shoulders,
I wiggle my nose.
Now all the wiggles are out of me,
I fold my hands and sit quietly.
Thank You, God,
for food and friends.

Margaret Coffman
Bremerton, Washington

*For Mother's love
and Father's care,
for food to eat and
clothes to wear,
for homes and friends and
answered prayers,
we thank You, God.*

Rose Burnett
Rocky Mount, North Carolina

*Jesus our Savior,
Lord of our lives,
please bless this food
and help us be wise.
In Jesus' name.
Amen.*

Jill Mauer
Osceola, Indiana

Hands up high (hands over head),
hands down low (at your sides);
hide those hands (behind your back)—
where'd they go?
Out comes one (one hand out front),
out comes two (the other out front);
clap them, fold them,
now we're through.
I fold my hands, I close my eyes
and let my thoughts to God arise.
Thank You for the world so sweet,
thank You for the food we eat;
thank You for the birds that sing,
thank You, God,
for everything.

L. Sylvester
Bel Air, Maryland